Children's Plays from Beatrix Potter

Children's Plays from Beatrix Potter

dramatized by
Rona Laurie

FREDERICK WARNE

First published in Great Britain by
Frederick Warne (Publishers) Ltd,
London, England, 1980

ISBN 0 7232 2488 9

Typeset by CCC, printed and bound in Great Britain by
William Clowes (Beccles) Limited,
Beccles and London

CONTENTS

PREFACE

I have adapted these short plays from the tales of Beatrix Potter with both informal and public performance in mind. On the one hand children can act them at home using the simplest presentation and improvising suggestions of costumes and properties. A piece of blue material tied round the head would serve for Jemima Puddle-Duck's bonnet, a bushy "tail" could be pinned on the child playing the Fox and the cast could assemble various odds and ends for Mrs Tiggy-Winkle's laundry.

On the other hand the scenes can be produced more formally, as a sequence or singly for a wider audience at a children's theatre performance, at a Festival or at a Junior School's Open Day.

I have tried to keep as faithfully as possible to the words in the original tales but occasionally slight alterations have been made to simplify the staging.

There is plenty of acting opportunity in the six plays for casts of varying numbers. As well as the speaking parts there are several non-speaking ones so that the younger members in the group may be included. For example, Miss Butterfly in "Mrs Tittlemouse" does not speak although she is seen tasting the sugar. Other characters have no actual lines to say but have been given expressive sounds, such as the grunts and squeals of Aunt Pettitoes' young family of pigs. Other non-speaking characters have been given an opportunity to mime, for instance at the end of "Ginger and Pickles" when the customers cram the shop at Henny-Penny's opening sale.

Sketch plans have been given as a guide to arranging the acting areas and furniture. It would be helpful to chalk out the various locations on a suitable floor. I am thinking particularly of the path to Mrs Tiggy-Winkle's door, the village street in "The Mystery of the Pie and the Patty-pan" and the geography of Mrs Tittlemouse's house.

A list of properties will be found at the beginning of each play. Some of these could be made by the children themselves, but, in the interests of fidelity to the original, Beatrix Potter's illustrations should be used as a guide. However, in informal productions improvised props would be acceptable or, indeed, they could be dispensed with altogether and mimed by the children.

When the young actors are bringing their characters to life in rehearsal they will find the pictures in the original tales an invaluable guide to characterization and movement.

Miss Potter herself is an important character. She not only introduces all the plays except "The Mystery of the Pie and the Patty-pan" but, if more than one is performed, acts as a unifying link. This part could usefully be played by the director of the play, be it a parent, teacher, professional director or an older child. Miss Potter could also act as prompter as she would, quite naturally, be looking at the book during the performance. The fact that her presence would reassure the more nervous members of the cast would be an added bonus.

I hope that children will enjoy acting these plays and that the contact with Beatrix Potter's fresh vision and fine use of the English language will prove of lasting value to them.

An exhibition of Beatrix Potter's drawings and paintings was held in London a few years ago and I have a vivid picture in my mind of enthusiasts of all ages, from seven to seventy and beyond, crowding the rooms and exclaiming with delight as they recognized their favourite characters ("Look, dear, here's Mrs Tiggy-Winkle!") ... I hope that the children who act in the plays in this book will be transported into that world of wonder that lasts a lifetime.

Mrs Tiggy-Winkle's Washing Day

CAST
(in order of appearance)

Miss Beatrix Potter
Kitten
Lucie
Sally Henny-Penny
Mrs Tiggy-Winkle
Peter Rabbit
Benjamin Bunny
Tom Titmouse
Cock Robin
Jenny Wren
Three Little Mice
Mole

LIST OF PROPERTIES

Book (Miss Potter)
Clothes props
Clothes lines
Clothes pegs
Clothes basket
2 irons
1 basin of starch
1 waistcoat (scarlet)
1 waistcoat (black velvet)
1 table-cloth
2 brown coats
3 pocket handkerchiefs

1 pinafore
1 pair yellow stockings
1 blue jacket
1 red handkerchief
1 pair mittens
2 shirt-fronts
4 woolly coats
1 tea-pot
2 cups and saucers
1 key
1 large safety-pin.
Turf for fire

The stage is divided into two acting areas. On the right is the farm area and on the left is Mrs Tiggy-Winkle's kitchen. They are connected by a winding path. Miss Potter sits at a small table with a book at the side of the stage. See plan:

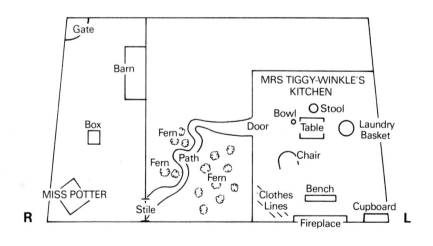

Miss Potter *(opening book)* Once upon a time there was a little girl called Lucie, who lived at a farm called Little-town. She was a good little girl – only she was always losing her pocket-handkerchiefs!

Lucie *(entering through farm-gate, crying)* I've lost my pocket-handkin! Three handkins and a pinny! Have *you* seen them, Tabby Kitten?

Kitten *(washing her white paws and ignoring Lucie)* Miaow . . . miaow.

Lucie Sally Henny-Penny, have *you* found three pocket-handkins?

Sally Henny-Penny *(running into barn, clucking)* I go barefoot, barefoot, barefoot!

(LUCIE mimes actions as MISS POTTER speaks:)

Miss Potter Lucie climbed upon the stile and looked up at the hill behind Little-town. And a great way up the hill-side she thought she saw some white things spread upon the grass. Lucie scrambled up the hill; she ran along a steep path-way. The path ended under a big rock. The grass was short and green, and there were clothes-props cut from bracken stems, with lines of plaited rushes, and a heap of tiny clothes pins – but no pocket-handkerchiefs! But there was a door!

(LUCIE standing outside hears MRS TIGGY-WINKLE singing inside her kitchen.)

Mrs Tiggy-Winkle

> Lily-white and clean, oh
> With little frills between, oh!
> Smooth and hot – red rusty spot
> Never here be seen, oh!

(LUCIE knocks at the door twice.)

Mrs Tiggy-Winkle *(in a little frightened voice)* Who's that?

Lucie *(entering)* Who are you? Have you seen my pocket-handkins?

Mrs Tiggy-Winkle *(staring anxiously at LUCIE and curtseying)* Oh, yes, if you please'm, I'm an excellent clear-starcher!

(She takes waist-coat from clothes-basket and spreads it on the ironing-blanket.)

Lucie *(sitting on stool)* What's that thing? That's not my pocket-handkin?

Mrs Tiggy-Winkle Oh no, if you please'm; that's a little scarlet waist-coat belonging to Cock Robin!

(She irons it and folds it and puts it on one side. Then she takes table-cloth from clothes-horse.)

Lucie That isn't my pinny?

Mrs Tiggy-Winkle Oh no, if you please'm; that's a damask table-cloth belonging to Jenny Wren; look how it's stained with currant wine! It's very bad to wash!

(She fetches another hot iron from the fire.)

Lucie   There's one of my pocket-handkins – and there's my pinny!

(MRS TIGGY-WINKLE irons it, and goffers it, and shakes out the frills.)

Lucie   Oh that *is* lovely!   What are those long yellow things with fingers like gloves!

Mrs Tiggy-Winkle   Oh, that's a pair of stockings belonging to Sally Henny-Penny – look how she's worn the heels out with scratching in the yard!   She'll very soon go barefoot!

Lucie   Why, there's another handkersniff – but it isn't mine; it's red.

Mrs Tiggy-Winkle   Oh no, if you please'm; that one belongs to old Mrs Rabbit; and it *did* so smell of onions!   I've had to wash it separately.   I can't get out the smell.

Lucie   There's another one of mine.

(MRS TIGGY-WINKLE takes mittens from clothes-basket.)

What are those funny little white things?

Mrs Tiggy-Winkle That's a pair of mittens belonging to Tabby Kitten; I only have to iron them; she washes them herself.

Lucie There's my last pocket-handkin!

(MRS TIGGY-WINKLE dips shirt-fronts into bowl on table.)

What are you dipping into the basin of starch?

Mrs Tiggy-Winkle They're little dicky shirt-fronts belonging to Tom Titmouse – most terrible particular! Now I've finished my ironing; I'm going to air some clothes.

(She starts to hang clothes on the airing-line.)

Lucie What are these dear soft fluffy things?

Mrs Tiggy-Winkle Oh those are woolly coats belonging to the little lambs at Skelghyl.

Lucie Will their jackets take off?

Mrs Tiggy-Winkle Oh yes, if you please'm; look at the sheep-mark on the shoulder. And here's one marked for Gatesgarth, and three that come from Little-town. They're *always* marked at washing!

(MRS TIGGY-WINKLE continues to hang up all sorts and sizes of clothes – and at last the basket is empty.)

Miss Potter Then Mrs Tiggy-Winkle made tea – a cup for herself and a cup for Lucie.

(MRS TIGGY-WINKLE makes a pot of tea and pours out two cups, humming a little tune. LUCIE and MRS TIGGY-WINKLE sit on the bench in front of the fire and drink their tea.)

When they had finished tea, they tied up the clothes in bundles; and Lucie's pocket-handkerchiefs were folded up inside her pinny, and fastened with a silver safety-pin.

(LUCIE and MRS TIGGY-WINKLE make up the fire, go out of the door, lock it and hide the key under the door-sill.)

Then away down the hill trotted Lucie and Mrs Tiggy-Winkle with the bundles of clothes. All the way down the path little animals came out of the fern to meet them.

(PETER RABBIT and BENJAMIN BUNNY come out of the fern L of the path.)

Mrs Tiggy-Winkle   Peter Rabbit, here is your blue jacket.   I am afraid it is very much shrunk.

Peter Rabbit   Thank you, Mrs Tiggy-Winkle.

Mrs Tiggy-Winkle   Benjamin Bunny, here is your aunt's red handkerchief; I'm afraid I couldn't get out the smell of onions.

17

Benjamin Bunny   Thank you, Mrs Tiggy-Winkle.

(The two rabbits disappear back into the fern.)

Mrs Tiggy-Winkle   If you please'm, I'll carry the bundle now.

(MRS TIGGY-WINKLE takes the washing from LUCIE.   They move further down the path.   TOM TITMOUSE, COCK ROBIN, JENNY WREN, THREE MICE and MOLE enter from fern L of path and form a circle round MRS TIGGY-WINKLE.)

Tom Titmouse, here are your dicky shirt-fronts starched most particular.

Tom Titmouse   Thank you, Mrs Tiggy-Winkle.

(He examines them carefully.)

Mrs Tiggy-Winkle   Cock Robin, here is your scarlet waist-coat.

Cock Robin   Thank you, Mrs Tiggy-Winkle.

Mrs Tiggy-Winkle   Jenny Wren, here is your damask table-cloth; it was stained with currant wine and very bad to wash.

Jenny Wren   Oh *thank* you, Mrs Tiggy-Winkle.

Mrs Tiggy-Winkle Here are your brown coats, Little Mice.

Three Little Mice *(in unison)* Thank you, Mrs Tiggy-Winkle.

Mrs Tiggy-Winkle Mole, here is your black velvet waist-coat.

Mole *(very quietly)* Thank you, Mrs Tiggy-Winkle.

(All the animals disappear into fern L of path.)

Lucie *(looking into bundle)* All that's left are my pinny and my three pocket-handkins; oh, and Sally Henny-Penny's stockings and Tabby Kitten's mittens. I will give them to them at the farm, Mrs Tiggy-Winkle.

Mrs Tiggy-Winkle Yes, if you please'm.

(They move to the stile and LUCIE scrambles on to it. She turns to say "Good-night".)

Lucie Good-night, good . . .

(She stops in surprise as MRS TIGGY-WINKLE starts running back up the path.)

Where is her white frilled cap? And her

shawl?   And her gown – and her petticoat?   And *how* small she has grown – and *how* brown – and covered with PRICKLES!   Why!   Mrs Tiggy-Winkle is nothing but a HEDGEHOG.

Miss Potter *(closing the book, rising and coming forward)*   Now some people say that little Lucie had been asleep upon the stile – but then how could she have found three clean pocket-handkins and a pinny, pinned with a silver safety-pin?   And besides – I have seen that door into the back of the hill called Cat Bells – and besides *I* am very well acquainted with dear Mrs Tiggy-Winkle!

Jemima Puddle-Duck and the Gentleman with Sandy Whiskers

CAST
(in order of appearance)

Miss Beatrix Potter
Jemima Puddle-Duck
Gentleman with Sandy Whiskers
Kep
Two Foxhound Puppies

LIST OF PROPERTIES

Book and pencil (Miss Potter)
Eggs (Jemima)
Newspaper (Gentleman with Sandy Whiskers)
Feathers in a sack (for nest)
Sage and onions (Jemima)

The stage is divided into two acting areas. On the right is a farm area and on the left is the clearing in the wood, where a GENTLEMAN WITH SANDY WHISKERS is sitting on a tree stump, reading a newspaper. Miss Potter sits at a small table with a book at the side of the stage. See plan:

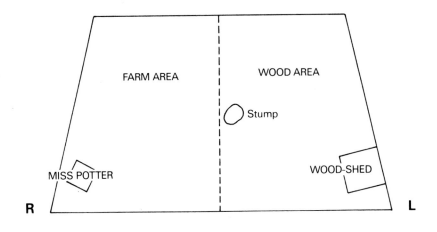

Miss Potter *(looking up from book, pencil in hand.)* Listen to the story of Jemima Puddle-Duck, who was annoyed because the farmer's wife would not let her hatch her own eggs.

(Enter Jemima Puddle-Duck.)

Jemima I wish to hatch my own eggs; I will hatch them all by myself.

Miss Potter She tried to hide her eggs; but they were always found and carried off. She determined to make a nest right away from the farm.

(JEMIMA leaves farm and approaches area of wood.)

She set off on a fine spring afternoon. When she reached the top of the hill, she saw a wood and an open space where the trees and brushwood had been cleared.

Jemima *(startled, seeing Gentleman with Sandy Whiskers)* Quack? Quack?

Gentleman with Sandy Whiskers *(looking over the top of his newspaper)* Madam, have you lost your way?

Jemima No, but I am trying to find a convenient, dry nesting-place.

Gentleman with Sandy Whiskers *(looking curiously
at Jemima)* Ah! is that so? Indeed!

Jemima   Yes.   I want to hatch out my own eggs, but they want one of the farm hens to sit on them.

Gentleman with Sandy Whiskers   Indeed! How interesting! I wish I could meet with that fowl.   I would teach it to mind its own business!   But as to a nest – there is no difficulty: I have a sackful of feathers in my wood-shed.

Jemima   But I would not like to be in anyone's way.

Gentleman with Sandy Whiskers   No, my dear madam, you will be in nobody's way.   You may sit there as long as you like.

(GENTLEMAN WITH SANDY WHISKERS leads JEMIMA to door of wood-shed.)

This is my summer residence; you would not find my earth – my winter house – so convenient.

(GENTLEMAN WITH SANDY WHISKERS shows JEMIMA in.)

Jemima   *(surprised)* What a vast quantity of feathers.   But it is very comfortable.

(After a short pause, while she is making her nest, JEMIMA comes out of the wood-shed.)

I have made my nest and now I am going home for the night.

Gentleman with Sandy Whiskers   What a pity you have to go.   But I promise to take great care of your nest until you come back again tomorrow.   I love eggs and ducklings and I shall be proud to see a fine nestful in my wood-shed.

(JEMIMA returns to farm.   While MISS POTTER is speaking JEMIMA goes twice to the wood-shed to lay her eggs – which she can carry with her in a bag hidden under her shawl.   When she leaves the wood-shed she looks very pleased with herself.)

Miss Potter   Jemima Puddle-Duck came every after-noon; she laid nine eggs in the nest.   The foxy gentleman admired them immensely.   He used to turn them over and count them when Jemima was not there.

(GENTLEMAN WITH SANDY WHISKERS mimes the action.)

(Enter JEMIMA.)

Jemima   I am going to begin to sit tomorrow and I will bring a bag of corn with me, so that I need never leave my nest until the eggs are hatched.   They might catch cold.

Gentleman with Sandy Whiskers Madam, I beg you not to trouble yourself with a bag; I will provide eats. But before you commence your tedious sitting, I intend to give you a treat. Let us have a dinner-party all to ourselves! May I ask you to bring up some herbs from the farm-garden to make a savoury omelette? Sage and thyme, and mint and two onions, and some parsley. I will provide lard for the stuff – lard for the omelette.

Miss Potter Jemima Puddle-Duck was a simpleton; not even the mention of sage and onions made her suspicious.

(JEMIMA returns to the farm where she meets Kep, the collie-dog.)

Kep What are you doing with those onions? Where do you go every afternoon by yourself, Jemima Puddle-Duck?

Jemima Since they will not let me hatch out my eggs myself, I have made a nest in the wood. A polite gentleman with sandy whiskers has allowed me to use his wood-shed.

Kep *(grinning)* Which wood do you mean?

Jemima The one you can see from the cart-road at the top of the hill.

Kep   And whereabouts in the wood is the shed, Jemima?

Jemima   In an open space in the middle.   Where are you off to, Kep?

Kep   To look for two fox-hound puppies – friends of mine.   I believe that they are out at walk with the butcher. *(Exit KEP.)*

(JEMIMA returns to the clearing in the wood.)

Gentleman with Sandy Whiskers *(glances uneasily round.   Abruptly)*   Come into the house as soon as you have looked at your eggs.   Give me the herbs for the omelette.   Be sharp!

(JEMIMA, surprised at his tone, goes into the shed.)

(Enter two FOXHOUND PUPPIES barking. They chase the GENTLEMAN WITH SANDY WHIS-KERS around the wooded area twice, and then offstage L.   There is a lot of baying and growling and squealing offstage.)

Miss Potter   And nothing more was ever seen of that foxy-whiskered gentleman.

(KEP dashes on and opens the door of the shed and lets out JEMIMA.   Then he escorts her back to the farm.)

Miss Potter *(closing the book, rising and coming forward)* Jemima laid some more eggs in June, and she was permitted to keep them herself; but only four of them hatched. Jemima Puddle-Duck said that it was because of her nerves; but she had always been a bad sitter.

Mrs Tittlemouse and the Uninvited Guest

CAST
(in order of appearance)

Miss Beatrix Potter
Mrs Tittlemouse
Beetle (non-speaking part)
Mother Ladybird (non-speaking part)
Spider
Babbitty Bumble
1st Bee
2nd Bee
3rd Bee
4th Bee
Mr Jackson
Miss Butterfly (non-speaking part)
Five Mice

LIST OF PROPERTIES

Book (Miss Potter)

Dustpan and brush (Mrs Tittlemouse)

Basket (Mrs Tittlemouse)

Mop (Mrs Tittlemouse)

Dishcloth (Mrs Tittlemouse)

Soft soap (Mrs Tittlemouse)

Flannel (Mrs Tittlemouse)

Scrubbing brush (Mrs Tittlemouse)

Beeswax polish (Mrs Tittlemouse)

Cherry-stones on plate

Thistle-down

Moss

Bees-nest

Lump sugar (Miss Butterfly)

Tin spoons

Acorn cups

Party food (Five Mice)

Twigs

Imagine that you are looking at a bank under a hedge. In the middle of the bank is the door of Mrs Tittlemouse's house and to the right of it her parlour window. You can see right into the house. In the seed-cellar is a BEETLE, in the pantry is a LADYBIRD, in the storeroom are four BEES. MRS TITTLEMOUSE is in the passage. See plan:

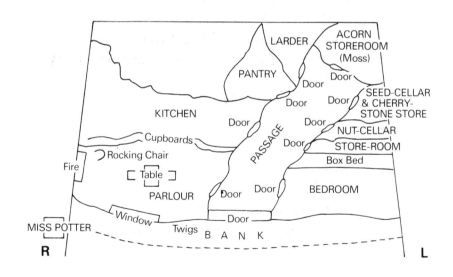

Miss Potter Once upon a time there was a wood-mouse, and her name was Mrs Tittlemouse.

(MRS TITTLEMOUSE opens her front-door and looks shyly out.)

Such a funny house!   There were yards and yards of sandy passages, leading to storerooms and nut-cellars and seed-cellars, all amongst the roots of the hedge.

(While MISS POTTER is speaking MRS TITTLE-MOUSE is opening the doors of her storerooms and cellars to inspect her stores.)

There was a kitchen, a parlour, a pantry, and a larder.   Also there was Mrs Tittlemouse's bed-room, where she slept in a little box bed!

(Having completed her rounds MRS TITTLE-MOUSE retires to bed.)

Mrs Tittlemouse was a most terribly tidy particular little mouse, always sweeping and dusting. Sometimes a beetle lost its way in the passages.

(Enter BEETLE from seed-cellar.)

Mrs Tittlemouse *(getting up and clattering her dust-pan)*   Shuh! shuh! little dirty feet!

Miss Potter One day a little old woman ran up and down in a red spotty cloak.

(Enter MOTHER LADYBIRD from pantry.)

Mrs Tittlemouse Your house is on fire, Mother Ladybird! Fly away home to your children!

(MRS TITTLEMOUSE shoos MOTHER LADYBIRD out of the window.)

(Enter SPIDER from L.)

Spider *(scuttling through front door)* Beg pardon, is this not Miss Muffet's?

Mrs Tittlemouse Go away, you bold bad spider! Leaving ends of cobweb all over my nice clean house!

(She bundles SPIDER out of the window.)

Now I must fetch cherry-stones and thistle-down seed for dinner.

(She starts to go to seed-cellar.)

I smell a smell of honey; is it the cowslips outside, in the hedge? I am sure I can see the marks of little dirty feet.

(Enter BABBITTY BUMBLE from R.)

Babbitty Bumble *(flying through window)* Zizz, Bizz, Bizzz!

Mrs Tittlemouse *(severely)* Good-day, Babbitty Bumble; I should be glad to buy some beeswax. But what are you doing down here? Why do you always come in at a window and say Zizz, Bizz, Bizzz?

Babbitty Bumble *(in a peevish squeak)* Zizz, Wizz, Wizzz!

(BABBITTY BUMBLE goes into acorn storeroom. MRS TITTLEMOUSE follows her and finds storeroom full of moss. She begins to pull it out. Four other BEES put their heads out.)

First Bee Buzz, Buzz!

Second Bee Buzz!

Third Bee Bizz, Wizz!

Fourth Bee Wizzz!

All Bees Buzz!

Mrs Tittlemouse I am not in the habit of letting

lodgings; this is an intrusion! I will have them turned out.

All Bees   Buzz! Buzz! Buzzz!

Mrs Tittlemouse   I wonder who would help me?

All Bees   Bizz, Wizz, Wizzz!

Mrs Tittlemouse   I will not have Mr Jackson; he never wipes his feet.

(MR JACKSON enters from L, comes through front door and into parlour.)

Mr Jackson   Ahem! Ahem! Ahem!

Mrs Tittlemouse   How do you do, Mr Jackson? Deary me, you have got very wet!

Mr Jackson *(smiling)*   Thank you, thank you, thank you, Mrs Tittlemouse! I'll sit awhile and dry myself.

(MRS TITTLEMOUSE goes round the parlour mopping up the water that has dripped from MR JACKSON'S coat tails.)

Mrs Tittlemouse   Will you take some dinner, Mr Jackson?

Mr Jackson   Thank you, thank you, Mrs Tittlemouse!

(He sits at the table.)

Mrs Tittlemouse   Would you like some cherry-stones, Mr Jackson?

Mr Jackson   Thank you, thank you, Mrs Tittle-mouse!   No teeth, no teeth, no teeth!

(He opens his mouth very wide.)

Mrs Tittlemouse   Would you like some thistle-down seed, Mr Jackson?

Mr Jackson *(blowing the thistle-down all over the room)*   Tiddly, widdly, widdly! Pouff, pouff, puff! Thank you, thank you, thank you, Mrs Tittlemouse!   Now what I really – *really* should like – would be a little dish of honey!

Mrs Tittlemouse   I am afraid I have not got any, Mr Jackson!

Mr Jackson *(smiling)*   Tiddly, widdly, widdly, Mrs Tittlemouse!   I can *smell* it; that is why I came to call.

(MR JACKSON begins to look into the cupboards and MRS TITTLEMOUSE follows him with a dish-

cloth to wipe his large wet footmarks off the floor.)

There is no honey here, Mrs Tittlemouse; perhaps there is some in the pantry?

Mrs Tittlemouse   Indeed, indeed, you will stick fast, Mr Jackson!

Mr   Jackson Tiddly,   widdly,   widdly,   Mrs Tittlemouse!

(MR JACKSON squeezes into the pantry.)

Tiddly, widdly, widdly?   No honey?   No honey? Mrs Tittlemouse?

(MR JACKSON squeezes into the larder.   MISS BUTTERFLY escapes and flies out of the window.)

Tiddly, widdly, widdly, Mrs Tittlemouse; you seem to have plenty of visitors!

Mrs Tittlemouse   And without any invitation!

Mr Jackson *(moving along the passage)*   Tiddly, widdly.

Babbity Bumble   Buzz!   Wizz!   Wizz!

(MR JACKSON goes to swallow BABBITTY, but changes his mind.)

Mr Jackson *(wiping his mouth with his coat-sleeve)* I do not like bumble bees.   They are all over bristles.

Babbity *(shrieking)*   Get out, you nasty old toad!

Mrs Tittlemouse   I shall go distracted!

(MRS TITTLEMOUSE shuts herself up in the nut-cellar and MR JACKSON pulls out the bees-nest and goes off with it L.)

Mrs Tittlemouse *(coming out of nut-cellar)*   Never did I see such a mess – smears of honey, and moss, and thistle-down – and marks of big and little dirty feet – all over my nice clean house!

(MRS TITTLEMOUSE goes out and fetches some twigs to partly close up the front door.)

I will make it too small for Mr Jackson!

Miss Potter *(as MRS TITTLEMOUSE mimes the actions)*   She fetched soft soap, and flannel, and a new scrubbing brush from the storeroom.   But she was too tired to do any more.   First she fell asleep in her chair, and then she went to bed.

Mrs Tittlemouse *(her head on the pillow)*   Will it ever be tidy again?

Miss Potter *(as MRS TITTLEMOUSE mimes the actions)* Next morning she got up very early and began spring cleaning. She swept, and scrubbed, and dusted; and she rubbed up the furniture with beeswax, and polished her little tin spoons. When it was all beautifully neat and clean, she gave a party to five other little mice, without Mr Jackson.

(Enter from L FIVE MICE. They are welcomed by MRS TITTLEMOUSE and led into the parlour. Enter from L MR JACKSON. He tries to squeeze in at the door.)

Mr Jackson Tiddly, widdly, widdly.

(MR JACKSON sits outside and the MICE hand him out acorn-cupfuls of honey-dew through the window.)

Your very good health, Mrs Tittlemouse!

(They all drink the health of MRS TITTLEMOUSE.)

All Mrs Tittlemouse!

Ginger and Pickles' Village Shop

CAST
(in order of appearance)

Miss Beatrix Potter
Ginger
Pickles
Peter Rabbit (non-speaking part)
Benjamin Bunny (non-speaking part)
Two Mice (non-speaking parts)
Mrs Tiggy-Winkle
Policeman (non-speaking part)
Sally Henny-Penny (non-speaking part)
Samuel Whiskers (non-speaking part)

(NOTE: More customers can be introduced in the last scene, for example Squirrel Nutkin, Jeremy Fisher, Jemima Puddle-Duck, Anna Maria and Old Mrs Rabbit.)

LIST OF PROPERTIES

Book (Miss Potter)
Shopping bag (Mrs Tiggy-
    Winkle)
Bar of soap
Book and pencil (Pickles)
Miscellaneous goods in the shop
Toffee
Candle in candle-stick
Cream crackers
Dried haddock
Account books

Bills
Envelope
Notebook (Policeman)
Rates and taxes bill
Gun (Pickles)
Rabbit-snare (Ginger)
Large printed poster (Henny-
    Penny)
Packet of snuff
Eggs
Biscuits

The stage is divided into two acting areas. On the L is Ginger and Pickles' shop and on the R is their back parlour. MISS POTTER sits with her book at a small table down R. GINGER sits L of table in back parlour and PICKLES sits R of it. See plan:

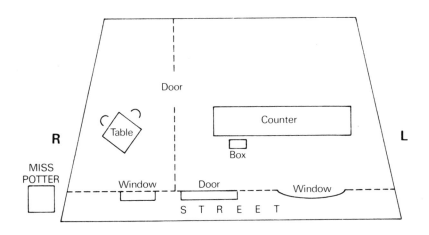

Miss Potter *(opening her book)*   Once upon a time there was a village shop.   The name over the window was "Ginger and Pickles".   Ginger and Pickles sold red spotty pocket-handerchiefs at a penny three farthings.   They also sold sugar, and snuff and galoshes.   In fact, although it was such a small shop it sold nearly everything – except a few things that you want in a hurry – like bootlaces, hair pins and mutton chops.   Ginger was a yellow tom-cat.

(Enter GINGER from back parlour.   He stands behind the counter.)

And Pickles was a terrier.

(Enter PICKLES from back parlour.   He stands at GINGER'S R.)

The rabbits were always a little bit afraid of Pickles.

(Enter PETER RABBIT and BENJAMIN BUNNY stage L.   They creep through shop door nervously.)

Pickles   Grrrr . . . grrr . . . grrr.

(PETER RABBIT and BENJAMIN BUNNY run out of shop.   Exit stage L.)

Miss Potter   The shop was also patronized by mice –

only the mice were rather afraid of Ginger.

(Enter TWO MICE stage R.   They tiptoe into shop.)

Ginger   Miaow ... please will you serve the mice, Pickles, because they make my mouth water.   I cannot bear to see them going out at the door carrying their little parcels.

(PICKLES serves them with biscuits and they scuttle out of shop.   Exit stage R.)

Pickles   I have the same feeling about rats, but it would never do to eat our own customers; they would leave us and go to Tabitha Twitchit's.

Ginger *(gloomily)*   On the contrary, they would go nowhere.

Miss Potter   Tabitha Twitchit kept the only other shop in the village. She did not give credit.   Ginger and Pickles gave unlimited credit.

(Enter MRS TIGGY-WINKLE from stage L.)

Mrs Tiggy-Winkle   A bar of soap if you please, Mr Pickles.

Pickles   Certainly, Mrs Tiggy-Winkle.

Mrs Tiggle-Winkle I will pay another time.

Pickles *(bowing low)* With pleasure, madam.

(PICKLES writes it down in a book as MRS TIGGY-WINKLE puts the soap in her shopping-bag and leaves the shop. Exit L.)

(PETER RABBIT and BENJAMIN BUNNY enter shop from stage L. GINGER serves them with toffee. Exit L.)

Miss Potter The customers came again and again, and bought quantities, in spite of being afraid of Ginger and Pickles. But there was no money in what was called the "till". Ginger and Pickles were obliged to eat their own goods. They ate them by candle-light after the shop was closed.

(PICKLES lights a candle and puts it on the counter, while GINGER puts up the shutters outside the shop window.)

Pickles ate biscuits.

(PICKLES sits on box by counter and eats cream crackers.)

Ginger ate a dried haddock.

(GINGER crouches on floor by counter to eat the fish.)

When it came to Jan. 1st there was still no money.

(GINGER takes down shutters and PICKLES blows out candle.)

Pickles I cannot buy my licence. It is very unpleasant. I am afraid of the police.

Ginger It is your own fault for being a terrier, *I* do not require a licence, and neither does Kep, the Collie dog.

Pickles It is very uncomfortable, I am afraid I shall be summoned. I have tried in vain to get a licence upon credit at the Post Office. The place is full of policemen. Let us send the bill again to Samuel

Whiskers, Ginger.   He owes 22/9 for bacon.

Ginger   I do not believe that he intends to pay at all.

Pickles   And I feel sure that Anna Maria pockets things – where are all the cream crackers?

Ginger   You have eaten them yourself.

(GINGER and PICKLES retire into the back parlour to do their accounts.   GINGER sits L of table and PICKLES R of it.   They add up sums, and sums, and sums.)

Ginger   Samuel Whiskers has run up a bill as long as his tail; he has had an ounce and three-quarters of snuff since October.

Pickles   What is seven pounds of butter at 1/3, and a stick of sealing wax and four matches?

Ginger   Send in all the bills again to everybody "with compts".

(There is a noise in the shop as a POLICEMAN enters L and puts an envelope on the counter.   PICKLES and GINGER come out of the back parlour.)

Pickles *(very agitated)*   Woof! woof! woof grrr!

Ginger *(spluttering)* Bite him, Pickles! Bite him! He's only a German doll!

(POLICEMAN continues writing in his notebook; twice he puts his pencil in his mouth, and once he dips it in the treacle.)

Pickles Woof! woof! woof! grrr! woof! woof! grrr!

(The POLICEMAN leaves the shop and exits stage L.)

Pickles Do you think he has gone to fetch a real live policeman? I am afraid it is a summons.

Ginger *(opening the envelope)* No, it is the rates and taxes, £3 19 11¾.

Pickles This is the last straw! Let us close the shop.

(They put up the shutters in front of the shop window and go off L.)

Miss Potter But they have not removed from the neighbourhood. In fact some people wish they had gone further. Ginger is living in the warren. I do not know what occupation he pursues; he looks stout and comfortable.

(GINGER strolls across the stage from L to R and

exits behind MISS POTTER.   A rabbit-snare hangs out of his pocket.)

Pickles is at present a gamekeeper.

(PICKLES enters stealthily from stage L.   He has a gun under his arm.   He crosses stage and exits behind MISS POTTER.)

The closing of the shop caused great inconvenience. So everybody was pleased when Sally Henny-Penny sent out a printed poster to say that she was going to re-open the shop.

(Enter SALLY HENNY-PENNY from L holding up a poster on which is written in large letters "Henny's Opening Sale! Grand Co-operative Jumble! Penny's penny prices! Come buy, come buy, come buy!" SALLY HENNY-PENNY goes into the shop.)

There was a rush upon the opening day.

(Enter from L SAMUEL WHISKERS, PETER RABBIT, BENJAMIN BUNNY, MRS TIGGY-WINKLE and TWO MICE.   They begin to buy the goods in the shop.   SAMUEL WHISKERS is first at the counter, holding an oblong packet of snuff, followed by MRS TIGGY-WINKLE who is buying eggs. PETER RABBIT and BENJAMIN BUNNY haven't got the right change.   The TWO MICE are

buying water biscuits, oatmeal wafers and cream crackers. More characters can appear – see cast.)

Sally Henny-Penny gets rather flustered when she tries to count out change, and insists on being paid cash; but she is quite harmless. And she has laid in a remarkable assortment of bargains. There is something to please everybody.

The Mystery of the Pie and the Patty-pan

CAST
(in order of appearance)

Ribby
Postman (non-speaking part)
Duchess
Tabitha Twitchit
Doctor Maggotty Magpie

LIST OF PROPERTIES

Letter ⎫
Quill pen ⎬ (Ribby)
Inkstand ⎭
Letter ⎫
Quill pen ⎬ (Duchess)
Inkstand ⎭
2 letters
2 identical pink and white pie-
   dishes containing pies
Basket and cloth (Ribby)
Basket and cloth (Duchess)
Tea-set
Tea-pot
Knives, forks and spoons
1 milk jug
1 butter dish (blue and white)
Coal

Hearth-brush
Can
Kettle
Table-cloth
1 packet tea (Tabitha Twitchit)
1 pound lump sugar (Tabitha)
1 pot of marmalade (Tabitha)
Muffins (Ribby)
Brush (Duchess)
Bunch of flowers (Duchess)
Bread pill (Dr Maggotty)
Shawl (Ribby)
Patty-pan
Bread and jam
Broken pie dish
Pail

The stage is divided into three unequal acting areas. At the R is Ribby's yard and house. Ribby's bedroom should be slightly higher than her kitchen/sitting room. Next comes Tabitha Twitchit's shop and, at stage L, is Duchess's house. The village street runs along the front of all three areas. See plan:

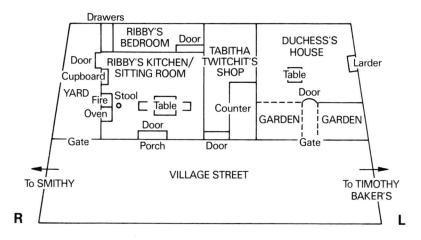

(RIBBY, a pussy-cat, is sitting at her table writing a letter and reading it aloud.)

Ribby   "Dear Duchess, will you come to tea with me today?   Come in good time, my dear Duchess, and we will have something so very nice.   I am baking it in a pie-dish – a pie-dish with a pink rim.   You never tasted anything so good!   And *you* shall eat it all!   I will eat muffins, my dear Duchess!"

(The POSTMAN arrives at RIBBY'S door.)

Ribby   Here is a letter for Duchess.

(POSTMAN touches his cap and goes off down the street and knocks at DUCHESS'S door.)

Duchess *(who is a little dog)*   A letter for me?   Thank you, Postman.

(DUCHESS opens the letter and reads it.   Then she goes into her house and writes a reply.)

Duchess *(writing and reading aloud)*   "My dear Ribby, I will come with much pleasure at a quarter past four.   But it is very strange. *I* was just going to invite you to come here, to supper, my dear Ribby, to eat something *most delicious*.   I will come very punctually, my dear Ribby."

(She pauses to think for a moment and then adds)

"I hope it isn't mouse?"   That does not look quite polite.

(She scratches out "isn't mouse".)

" I hope it will be fine."

(She goes to her front door, sees the POSTMAN passing her gate and gives him the letter.)

Will you please deliver this to Mrs Ribston?

(POSTMAN touches his cap and goes into TABITHA'S shop.   DUCHESS goes into her house and reads Ribby's letter again.)

(DUCHESS talks to herself)   I am dreadfully afraid it *will* be mouse!   I really couldn't, *couldn't* eat mouse pie.   And I shall have to eat it, because it is a party.   And *my* pie was going to be veal and ham.   A pink and white pie-dish!   And so is mine; just like Ribby's dishes; they were both bought at Tabitha Twitchit's.

(She goes into her larder, takes the pie off a shelf and looks at it.)

It is all ready to put into the oven.   Such a lovely

pie-crust; and I put in a little tin patty-pan to hold up the crust; and I made a hole in the middle with a fork to let out the steam – Oh I do wish I could eat my own pie, instead of a pie made of mouse!

(She goes to her table and reads Ribby's letter again.)

"A pink and white pie-dish – and *you* shall eat it *all*." "You" means me – then Ribby is not going to even taste the pie herself? A pink and white pie-dish! Ribby is sure to go out to buy the muffins . . . Oh what a good idea!

(She jumps up, delighted with her own cleverness.)

Why shouldn't I rush along and put my pie into Ribby's oven when Ribby isn't there?

(DUCHESS goes to back of her house to find a basket for the pie. POSTMAN comes out of MRS TABITHA TWITCHIT'S shop, goes to RIBBY'S door and knocks on it.)

Ribby *(at door)* Thank you; it is Duchess's reply.

(POSTMAN touches his cap and goes off stage R. RIBBY goes into her house and reads letter.)

Good! Ribby can come to tea. I must pop my pie into the oven.

(She fetches it from back of kitchen.)

I'll put it into the lower oven; the top oven bakes too quickly.

(She has some difficulty in opening the lower oven door.)

But this door is very stiff.

(She puts pie in lower oven.)

It is a pie of the most delicate and tender mouse minced up with bacon.   And I have taken out all the bones; because Duchess did nearly choke herself with a fish-bone last time I gave a party.   She eats a little fast – rather big mouthfuls.   But a most genteel and elegant little dog; infinitely superior company to Cousin Tabitha Twitchit.

(RIBBY puts on some coal and sweeps up the hearth.   Then she goes out through the back door with a can to the well in the yard, for water to fill up the kettle.   She fills kettle, then shakes mats out at the front-door.   She polishes the table and two chairs, then spreads the tablecloth and sets table with her best china tea-set which she takes out of cupboard near the fireplace.   She peeps into bottom oven.)

The pie looks very comfortable.

(She takes her shawl and bonnet from a hook by the front-door. She puts them on, picks up a basket and goes to TABITHA TWITCHIT's shop.)

Duchess *(coming out of her gate)* Oh dear! There is Ribby! I will just bow to her. We must not speak because we are going to have a party.

(DUCHESS and RIBBY bow to each other as they pass. RIBBY goes to TABITHA'S shop. DUCHESS runs round corner to RIBBY'S back-door.)

Ribby Good afternoon, Cousin Tabitha. I want a packet of tea – the best, if you please. I have asked Duchess to tea.

Tabitha *(sniffing disdainfully)*   Anything else?

Ribby   A pound of lump sugar, and a pot of marmalade.

Tabitha   Give me your basket and I will put them in.

Ribby   Thank you, Cousin Tabitha.

(They start to gossip in low voices. DUCHESS enters through the back-door of RIBBY'S house. She goes straight to the oven and turns the handle of the bottom door but it will not open.)

Duchess   I think this handle is a sham.

(She tries the top handle ; the oven-door opens.)

It is a very odd thing that Ribby's pie isn't here.   But I will put mine in.   It is nice and hot.

(She puts her pie in the top oven and closes the door.)

Now I must try to find the pie made of mouse.

(She searches the china cupboard and then goes upstairs to look in RIBBY'S chest of drawers.   RIBBY comes out of TABITHA'S shop.)

Ribby That was a pleasant gossip, Cousin Tabitha. Now I must go to Timothy Baker's for the muffins for tea.

(She goes off stage L.)

Tabitha *(looking after her)* Goodbye, Ribby. *(To herself, disdainfully)* A little *dog* indeed! Just as if there were no CATS in Sawrey! And a *pie* for afternoon tea! The very idea!

(TABITHA goes back into her shop. RIBBY enters with the muffins from stage L. Then goes back home. As she enters the front porch, DUCHESS who is in the bedroom, hears her and runs downstairs and out of the back-door.)

Ribby *(coming into the kitchen)* What is that sort of scuffling noise at the back of the house? *(Loudly)* Who is there? I trust it is not that pie: the spoons are locked up, however.

(RIBBY opens the bottom oven door with some difficulty and turns the pie. DUCHESS creeps out of the yard and returns down the street home.)

Duchess Now I must get ready for the party. Where is my brush?

(She starts to brush her black coat.)

Ribby *(looking in china cupboard)* There is no one hiding in here. Now I must change my dress for the party.

(RIBBY goes to her bedroom.)

I will wear my lilac silk and my embroidered muslin apron and tippet.

(RIBBY puts them on and then turns to her chest of drawers: she is surprised.)

It is very strange, I did not *think* I left that drawer pulled out; has somebody been trying on my mittens?

(RIBBY comes downstairs and makes the tea, and puts the teapot on the hob. She peeps again into the bottom oven.)

The pie is a lovely brown and it is steaming hot.

(RIBBY sits down before the fire to wait for DUCHESS.)

I am glad I used the bottom oven, the top one would certainly have been very much too hot. I wonder why this cupboard door was open? Can there really have been someone in the house?

(RIBBY dozes by the fire.)

Duchess *(coming out of her house)*   I will pick a bunch of flowers as a present for Ribby.   *(She does so.)*

It is time to go.

(She starts down street.)

I wonder if Ribby has taken *my* pie out of the oven yet?   And whatever can have become of the other pie made of mouse?

(She arrives at RIBBY'S porch and taps at her door.)

Is Mrs Ribston at home?

Ribby *(waking with a start and coming to the door)*   Come in!   And how do you do, my dear Duchess?   I hope I see you well?

Duchess   Quite well, I thank you, and how do *you* do, my dear Ribby?   I've brought you some flowers; what a delicious smell of pie!

Ribby *(taking flowers)*   Oh, what lovely flowers.   Yes, it is mouse and bacon!

Duchess   Do not talk about food, my dear Ribby; what a lovely white tea-cloth!... Is it done to a turn? Is it still in the oven?

Ribby I think it wants another five minutes, just a
shade longer; I will pour out the tea, while we
wait. Do you take sugar, my dear Duchess?

Duchess Oh yes, please, my dear Ribby; and may I
have a lump upon my nose?

Ribby *(putting sugar on DUCHESS'S nose)* With
pleasure, my dear Duchess; how beautifully you
beg! Oh, how sweetly pretty!

Duchess *(sniffing)* How good that pie smells! I do
love veal and ham – I mean to say mouse and
bacon –

(DUCHESS drops the sugar in confusion and has to go hunting under the tea-table, so she does not see which oven RIBBY opens in order to get out the pie. RIBBY sets the pie on the table. They sit down.)

Ribby   I will first cut the pie for you; I am going to have muffin and marmalade.

Duchess   Do you really prefer muffin?   Mind the patty-pan.

Ribby   I beg your pardon?

Duchess *(hurriedly)*   May I pass you the marmalade?

(They eat in silence.   The muffins and helping of pie disappear.)

Ribby   I will fill up the tea-pot.

(RIBBY goes to the hob.)

Duchess *(aside)*   I think – I *think* it would be wiser if I helped myself to pie; though Ribby did not seem to notice anything when she was cutting it.   What very small fine pieces it has cooked into!   I do not remember that I had minced it up so fine; I suppose this is a quicker oven than my own.

Ribby *(aside, at hob)*   How fast Duchess is eating!

(RIBBY comes to the table with the tea-pot.)

A little more bacon, my dear Duchess?

Duchess *(fumbling with her spoon)*   Thank you, my dear Ribby; I was only feeling for the patty-pan.

Ribby   The patty-pan; my dear Duchess?

Duchess *(blushing)*   The patty-pan that held up the pie-crust.

Ribby   Oh, I didn't put one in, my dear Duchess.   I don't think that it is necessary in pies made of mouse.

Duchess *(anxiously fumbling with her spoon)*   I can't find it!

Ribby *(perplexed)*   There isn't a patty-pan.

Duchess   Yes, indeed, my dear Ribby.   Where can it have gone to?

Ribby   There most certainly is not one, my dear Duchess.   I disapprove of tin articles in puddings and pies. It is most undesirable –*(in a lower voice)*   especially when people swallow in lumps!

(DUCHESS, looking very much alarmed, continues to scoop the inside of the pie-dish.)

My Great-aunt Squintina (grandmother of Cousin Tabitha Twitchit) died of a thimble in a Christmas plum-pudding.   *I* never put any article of metal in *my* puddings or pies.

(DUCHESS looks aghast and tilts up the pie-dish.)

I have only four patty-pans, and they are all in the cupboard.

Duchess *(howling)*   I shall die!   I shall die!   I have swallowed a patty-pan!   Oh, my dear Ribby, I do feel so ill!

Ribby   It is impossible, my dear Duchess; there was not a patty-pan.

Duchess   *(moaning and whining and rocking herself about)*   Oh, I feel so dreadful.   I have swallowed a patty-pan!

Ribby *(severely)*   There was *nothing* in the pie.

Duchess   Yes there *was*, my dear Ribby.   I am sure I have swallowed it!

Ribby   Let me prop you up with a pillow, my dear

Duchess.   Where do you think you feel it?

Duchess   Oh, I do feel so ill *all over* me, my dear Ribby!   I have swallowed a large tin patty-pan with a sharp scalloped edge!

Ribby   Shall I run for the doctor?   I will just lock up the spoons!

Duchess   Oh, yes, yes!   Fetch Dr. Maggotty, my dear Ribby.   He is a Pie himself; he will certainly understand.

(RIBBY settles DUCHESS in an arm-chair before the fire and hurries off stage R to find the DOC-TOR.   She finds him at the smithy.)

Duchess *(sighing and groaning)*   How *could* I have swallowed it!   Such a large thing as a patty-pan!

(She gets up and goes to the table and feels inside the pie-dish again with a spoon.)

No; there is no patty-pan, and I put one in; and nobody has eaten pie except me, so I must have swallowed it!

(She sits down again and stares mournfully at the grate.   Suddenly she smells something and hears something go sizz-z-zle in the oven.   She opens the

door of the top oven.   There stands the pie.)

There is my veal and ham pie and there is the patty-pan; I can see it through the pie-crust. Then I must have been eating MOUSE!... No wonder I feel ill... But perhaps I should feel worse if I had really swallowed a patty-pan! What a very awkward thing to have to explain to Ribby!   I think I will put *my* pie in the back-yard and say nothing about it.   When I go home, I will run round and take it away.

(DUCHESS puts her pie outside the back-door, sits down again by the fire and shuts her eyes.)

Doctor Maggotty *(entering with RIBBY stage R)* Gammon? Ha! HA!

Ribby Come quickly, Doctor, my guest has swallowed a patty-pan.

Doctor Maggotty *(his head on one side)* Spinach? Ha HA!

(As they hurry down the village street, TABITHA TWITCHIT puts her head round her shop-door.)

Tabitha I *knew* they would over-eat themselves!

(RIBBY and DOCTOR MAGGOTTY go into

RIBBY'S house.   DUCHESS seems fast asleep.)

Doctor Maggotty   Gammon, ha, HA?

Duchess *(waking up with a jump)*   I am feeling very much better.

Ribby   I am truly glad to hear it!   He has brought you a pill, my dear Duchess!

Duchess *(backing away from DOCTOR MAG-GOTTY)*   I think I should feel *quite* well if he only felt my pulse.

Ribby   It is only a bread pill. You had much better take it; drink a little milk, my dear Duchess!

Doctor Maggotty *(giving DUCHESS a pill)* Gammon?   Gammon?

(DUCHESS coughs and chokes.)

Ribby *(losing her temper)* Don't say that again!   Here, take this bread and jam, and get out into the yard.

(DOCTOR MAGGOTTY sidles outside back-door.)

Doctor Maggotty *(shouting triumphantly)*   Gammon and Spinach!   Ha ha HA!

Duchess I am feeling very much better, my dear Ribby. Do you not think that I had better go home before it gets dark?

Ribby Perhaps it might be wise, my dear Duchess. I will lend you a nice warm shawl *(she gets one from the hook beside the door)*, and you shall take my arm.

Duchess I would not trouble you for worlds! I feel wonderfully better. One pill of Dr Maggotty –

Ribby Indeed it is most admirable, if it has cured you of a patty-pan! I will call directly after breakfast to ask how you have slept. Good-bye, my dear Duchess.

Duchess *(leaving)* Good-bye, my dear Ribby.

(RIBBY goes in and shuts her door. DUCHESS runs round to the back of RIBBY'S house and peeps into the yard. Dr MAGGOTTY is drinking gravy out of a patty-pan.)

Doctor Maggotty *(shouting at DUCHESS)* Gammon, ha, HA!

(DUCHESS runs home.)

Ribby Well, I must get some water to wash up the tea-things.

69

(She goes out of the back-door with a pail.   She sees a pink and white pie-dish lying smashed in the middle of the yard and a patty-pan under the pump.)

(She gasps in amazement)   Did you ever see the like!   So there really *was* a patty-pan? . . . But *my* patty-pans are all in the kitchen cupboard.   Well I never did! . . . Next time I want to give a party – I will invite Cousin Tabitha Twitchit!

Pigling Bland and Pig-Wig

CAST
(in order of appearance)

Miss Beatrix Potter
Aunt Pettitoes
Cross-patch
Suck-suck
Yock-yock
Spot
Alexander
Pigling Bland
Chin-chin
Stumpy
Policeman
Hen
Cockerel
Broody Hen
Mr Piperson
Pig-wig
Grocer

LIST OF PROPERTIES

2 clothes brushes (Miss Potter and Aunt Pettitoes)

1 large pocket handkerchief (Aunt Pettitoes)

2 pig licences (Miss Potter)

2 large safety pins (Miss Potter)

2 bundles tied up in red and white handkerchiefs

2 small sticks

Conversation peppermints in screws of paper (Miss Potter)

Notebook (Policeman)

Porridge pot and meal (Mr Piperson)

3 plates

3 spoons

1 hamper (Mr Piperson)

1 bucket

1 dishcloth (Pigling Bland)

1 hearth brush (Pigling Bland)

1 antimacassar

Newspaper (Grocer)

The stage is divided into three acting areas of unequal size. To the R is the farmhouse yard, in the middle the roads meet at the cross-roads stage C and to the L is MR PIPERSON'S kitchen. A road runs along the front of the acting areas. See plan:

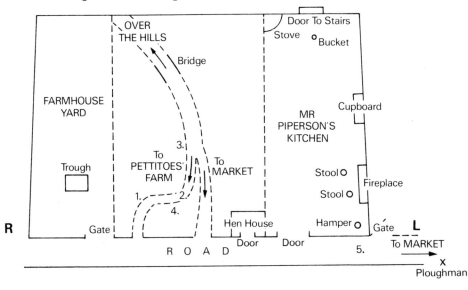

1. Picnic place   2. Encounter with policeman   3. Cross-roads   4. Wooded area   5. Encounter with grocer

Scene One

Miss Potter *(entering from farmhouse up R)* Once upon a time there was an old pig called Aunt Pettitoes.

(AUNT PETTITOES enters from down R. She is followed at intervals by her family.)

She had eight of a family: four little girl pigs . . .

Aunt Pettitoes *(calling her on)* Cross-patch!

(Enter CROSS-PATCH, scowling.)

Cross-patch Umph, umph.

(She goes to trough.)

Aunt Pettitoes Suck-suck!

(Enter SUCK-SUCK. She goes to trough making sucking noises.)

Yock-yock!

(Enter YOCK-YOCK at a run.)

Yock-yock Umph, umph, yock, yock.

Aunt Pettitoes   Spot!

(Enter SPOT.   She is the smallest.)

Miss Potter   . . . and four little boy pigs.

Aunt Pettitoes   Alexander!

(ALEXANDER enters squealing and rushes greedily to the trough, pushing the four little girl pigs aside.)

Aunt Pettitoes   Pigling Bland!

(Enter PIGLING BLAND more sedately.   He goes to trough.)

Pigling Bland   Umph, umph . . .

Aunt Pettitoes   Chin-chin!

(Enter CHIN-CHIN.)

Chin-chin   Umph, umph . . .

(He goes to trough.)

Aunt Pettitoes   Stumpy!

(Enter STUMPY with a rush.)

Stumpy   Umph, umph, umph.

(He tries to push in at the trough.)

Miss Potter   The eight little pigs had very fine appetites.

Aunt Pettitoes *(proudly)*   Yus, yus, yus!   They eat and indeed they *do* eat!

(There are fearful squeals; ALEXANDER has squeezed inside the hoops of the trough and stuck.   MISS POTTER and AUNT PETTITOES drag him out by the hind legs.   When they have rescued him AUNT PETTITOES shoos her family out of the yard stage R.)

Miss Potter   Aunt Pettitoes, Aunt Pettitoes ... you are a worthy person, but your family is not well brought up.   Every one of them has been in mischief except Spot and Pigling Bland.

Aunt Pettitoes *(sighing)*   Yus, yus!

Miss Potter   And they drink bucketfuls of milk; I shall have to get another cow!   Good little Spot shall stay at home to do the house-work; but the others must go.   Four little boy pigs and four little girl pigs are too many altogether.

Aunt Pettitoes   Yus, yus, yus, there will be more to eat without them.

Miss Potter   I shall send Chin-chin and Suck-suck away in a wheelbarrow, and Stumpy, Yock-yock and Cross-patch away in a cart. Pigling Bland and Alexander will go to market.

(Enter PIGLING BLAND and ALEXANDER. MISS POTTER and AUNT PETTITOES brush their coats, curl their tails and wash their faces.)

Aunt Pettitoes *(wiping her eyes)*   Now Pigling Bland, son Pigling Bland, you must go to market.   Take your brother Alexander by the hand.   Mind your Sunday clothes, and remember to blow your nose.   Beware of traps, hen roosts, bacon and eggs; always walk upon your hind legs.

(PIGLING BLAND looks solemnly at his mother.)

Now son Alexander take the hand –

Alexander *(giggling)*   Wee, wee, wee!

Aunt Pettitoes   Take the hand of your brother Pigling Bland.   You must go to market.   Mind –

Alexander *(interrupting again)*   Wee, wee, wee!

Aunt Pettitoes   You put me out – observe sign-posts and milestones; do not gobble herring bones –

Miss Potter *(impressively)*   And remember, if you once cross the county boundary you cannot come back.   Alexander, you are not attending.   Here are two licences permitting two pigs to go to market in Lancashire.   Attend, Alexander.   *(To AUNT PETTITOES)*   He is hopelessly volatile.   I have had no end of trouble in getting these papers from the policeman.

(MISS POTTER pins the papers inside their waistcoat pockets.)

Aunt Pettitoes   Here are your bundles and conversation peppermints.

(MISS POTTER and AUNT PETTITOES see them off at the gate.)

Miss Potter } Goodbye, Pigling Bland.   Goodbye,
Aunt Pettitoes } Alexander!

(MISS POTTER and AUNT PETTITOES exit into farm-house.   PIGLING BLAND and ALEXANDER start off along the road.)

Alexander *(dancing, pinching his brother and singing.)*
This pig went to market,
This pig stayed at home,
This pig had a bit of meat –

Let's see what they have given *us* for dinner, Pigling?

(They sit down and untie their bundles.   ALEXANDER gobbles up his dinner and all his peppermints.)

Give me one of your peppermints, please, Pigling.

Pigling Bland *(doubtfully)*   But I wish to preserve them for emergencies.

Alexander *(squealing with laughter)*   Wee, wee, wee!

(ALEXANDER pricks PIGLING with the pin that had fastened his pig paper; PIGLING slaps

him; ALEXANDER drops pin and tries to take PIGLING'S pin. The papers get mixed up.)

Pigling Bland *(reprovingly)* You are not behaving well, Alexander.

(They make up their differences by patting each other on the back and continue along the road.)

Pigling Bland ⎫
Alexander ⎭ *(singing)*

    Tom, Tom, the piper's son,
    Stole a pig and away he ran!
    But all the tune that he could play,
    Was "Over the hills and far away".

Policeman *(who has entered from back, down 'Over the Hills' road)* What's that, young sirs? Stole a pig? *(He takes out his note-book.)* Where are your licences?

Pigling Bland *(handing him his paper)* Here you are, Mr Policeman.

Alexander *(after fumbling in pocket, hands over something scrumply)* Here you are, Mr Policeman.

Policeman *(reading)* "To 2½ oz conversation sweeties at three farthings" – What's this? This ain't a licence.

79

Alexander   I had one, indeed I had, Mr Policeman!

Policeman   It's not likely they let you start without.   I am passing the farm.   You may walk with me.

Pigling Bland   Can I come back too?

Policeman   I see no reason, young sir.   Your paper is all right.

(PIGLING BLAND gives ALEXANDER a peppermint and sits forlornly by the roadside watching them walk back towards the farm.)

(The POLICEMAN leads ALEXANDER back to the farm, through the yard and off the stage R.)

Miss Potter *(entering from R)*   They arrived about tea time. I disposed of Alexander in the neighbourhood; he did fairly well when he had settled down.

END OF SCENE ONE

SCENE TWO

(Hens and cockerel are already inside hen house, downstage, L C. Pig-wig is inside cupboard, upstage L. Pigling Bland is seated by roadside at 2. (See plan.) PIGLING BLAND gets up dejectedly and goes along road until he comes to cross-roads and a sign-post.)

Pigling Bland *(reading aloud)*   "To Market Town, 5 Miles", "Over the Hills, 4 miles", "To Pettitoes Farm, 3 miles".

(He chooses road to Market Town.)

I have never wanted to go to market to stand all by myself, to be stared at, pushed, and hired by some big strange farmer.   I wish I could have a little garden and grow potatoes.

(He puts his hand in his pocket and feels another paper.)

(squealing)   Alexander's licence!

(PIGLING BLAND runs back frantically, hoping to overtake ALEXANDER and the POLICEMAN but he takes a wrong turn and is quite lost in a wooded area.)

(frightened)   Wee, wee, wee!   I can't find my way home!

(PIGLING BLAND finds a small hut and creeps inside.)

I am afraid it *is* a hen house, but what can I do?

Hen *(inside hen house, clucking)*   Bacon and eggs, bacon and eggs!

Cockerel *(inside, scolding)*   Trap, trap, trap, cackle, cackle, cackle!

Broody Hen *(inside, clucking)*   To market, to market! Jiggety jig!

(MR PIPERSON enters from back, L, through door to stairs.   He goes into the hen house.)

Hens and Cockerel *(inside)*   Cackle, cackle, cackle.

Mr Piperson *(inside)*   Hello, here's another.

(MR PIPERSON comes out of the hen house leading PIGLING BLAND by the ear.   He opens door of his kitchen and enters with PIGLING.)

Mr Piperson *(grinning and turning PIGLING'S pockets inside out without finding his papers and peppermints* *which he has hidden in his clothes.)*

This one's come of himself, whatever.

(MR PIPERSON puts a pot on the fire and unlaces his boots. PIGLING sits on stool by fire and warms his hands. MR PIPERSON throws a boot at a cupboard.)

Pig-wig *(in cupboard)* Snuffle, snuffle, snuffle!

Mr Piperson Shut up!

(MR PIPERSON throws second boot at cupboard.)

Pig-wig *(in cupboard)* Snuffle, snuffle, snuffle!

Mr Piperson Be quiet, will ye?

(MR PIPERSON makes porridge for three; one plateful he gives to PIGLING, one he takes himself and the third he puts in cupboard and locks up.)

Mr Piperson *(finishing his porridge)* You may sleep on the rug.

(MR PIPERSON goes up to bed through door at the back of the kitchen. PIGLING sleeps on the rug, snoring gently.)

(A short pause.)

(Enter MR PIPERSON.   He makes more porridge.)

Mr Piperson   It's warmer this morning.   Wake up, will ye?   You'll likely be moving on again?

(There is a whistle from the gate.   MR PIPERSON picks up a hamper.)

Now shut the door behind me and mind ye don't meddle with nought or I'll come back and skin ye!

(He hurries out to waiting cart at his gate, downstage L. Exit.)

PIGLING finishes his porridge and washes up the plates in a bucket.)

Pigling Bland *(singing)*
>Tom with his pipe made such a noise,
>He called up all the girls and boys –
>And they all ran to hear him play
>"Over the hills and far away".

Pig-wig *(inside the cupboard in a little smothered voice)*
>Over the hills and a great way off,
>The wind shall blow my top knot off!

(PIGLING goes to door of locked cupboard and snuffs at the keyhole. Silence. He pushes a peppermint under the door. It is sucked in immediately. He pushes in all the remaining six peppermints, one by one. He then brushes up the hearth, puts on the pot to boil and goes to his stool by the fire where he falls asleep waiting for MR PIPERSON to return.)

Mr Piperson *(entering, downstage L, very affable)* Wake up, will ye? *He slaps PIGLING on the back.)* Are ye hungry? I'll heat up the porridge for our suppers.

(He hands PIGLING a plateful, takes one himself and puts a third into the cupboard.)

Pig-wig *(in cupboard)* Snuffle, snuffle, snuffle.

(MR PIPERSON locks the cupboard door but without properly shutting it.)

Mr Piperson Well, I'm off to bed. Now don't ye go waking me before twelve.

(MR PIPERSON goes up to bed.)

Pig-wig *(coming out of cupboard and standing by PIGLING'S stool.)* My name is Pig-wig. Make me more porridge, please!

(PIG-WIG points at PIGLING'S plate and he gives it to her.   Then he helps himself to meal and makes some more porridge.)

Pigling Bland   How did you come here?

Pig-wig *(with her mouth full)*   Stolen.

Pigling Bland   What for?

Pig-wig *(cheerfully)*   Bacon, hams.

Pigling Bland *(horrified)*   Why on earth don't you run away?

Pig-wig *(decidedly)*   I shall after supper.

(PIGLING hands her a second plate of porridge.)

Pigling Bland   You can't go in the dark.   Do you know your way by daylight?

Pig-wig *(looking anxious)*   I know we can see this little white house from the hills across the river.   Which way are *you* going, Mr Pig?

Pigling Bland   To market – I have two pig papers.   I might take you if you have no objection.

Pig-wig   Thank you, thank you, Mr Pig.   When can

we start?   Can we start now?

(PIGLING becomes embarrassed; he shuts his eyes and pretends to go to sleep on his stool.   PIG-WIG starts to eat peppermints.)

Pigling Bland *(opening his eyes)*   I thought you had eaten the peppermints.

Pig-wig *(studying what is written on them)*   Only the corners.

Pigling Bland *(alarmed)*   I wish you wouldn't.   He might smell them through the ceiling.

Pig-wig *(returning the peppermints to her pocket)*   Sing something.

Pigling Bland *(much dismayed)*   I am sorry . . . I have
   toothache.

Pig-wig   Then I will sing.   You will not mind if I say
   iddy tidditty?   I have forgotten some of the words.

Pigling Bland   Of course not.

Pig-wig *(clapping time and singing)*
   A funny old mother pig lived in a
      stye, and three little piggies had she;
   (Ti idditty idditty) umph, umph,
      umph! and the little pigs said, wee
      wee!

   *(As she sings her head nods lower and lower and her
   eyes close up.)*

   Those three little piggies, grew peaky
      and lean, and lean they might very
      well be;
   For somehow they couldn't say umph,
      umph, umph! and they wouldn't
      say wee, wee, wee,
   For somehow they couldn't say –

   *(PIG-WIG rolls over, fast asleep on the hearth-
   rug. PIGLING covers her up with an
   antimacassar. They both rest but PIGLING is*

afraid to go to sleep. The cockerel from henhouse crows. PIGLING ties up his bundle.)

Pigling Bland Wake up, Pig-wig; it is time to go.

Pig-wig *(excited and half-frightened)* But it's dark. How can we find our way?

Pigling Bland The cock has crowed; we must start before the hens come out; they might shout up to Mr Piperson.

Pig-wig *(sitting down again and starting to cry)* Oh dear, oh dear!

Pigling Bland Come away Pig-wig; we can see when we get used to it.   Come!

(Hens start clucking.)

I can hear them clucking!

(PIGLING opens the house door quietly and they slip away hand in hand along the road that leads to the market.   PIG-WIG starts to dance.)

Pig-wig *(singing)*
      Tom, Tom, the piper's son, stole a pig
        and away he ran!
      But all the tune that he could play,
        was "Over the hills and far away"!

Pigling Bland Come, Pig-wig, we must get there before folks are stirring.

Pig-wig Why do you want to go to market, Pigling?

Pigling Bland I don't want; I want to grow potatoes.

Pig-wig Have a peppermint?

Pigling Bland *(quite crossly)*   I don't want one.

Pig-wig Does your poor toothy hurt?

Pigling Bland   Umph.

(PIG-WIG eats the peppermint herself.)

Pigling Bland   Pig-wig! come quickly, there's a man ploughing; over there.

(They hurry on but suddenly PIGLING stops.   He sees a GROCER coming towards them from stage L.)

Pigling Bland   Take that peppermint out of your mouth, Pig-wig, we may have to run.   Don't say one word.   Leave it to me.

PIGLING begins to walk lame, holding PIG-WIG'S arm.)

Grocer   Hello!   Where are *you* going to?

(PIGLING stares at him vacantly.)

Are you deaf?   Are you going to market?

(PIGLING nods slowly.)

I thought as much.   It was yesterday.   Show me your licence? *(more loudly)*   Papers?   Pig licence?

(PIGLING fumbles in all his pockets and hands up the papers.)

This here is a young lady; is her name Alexander?

Pigling Bland *(coughing asthmatically)*   Ahem, ahem!

Grocer *(producing newspaper from his pocket and turning to the advertisement column)* "Lost, stolen or strayed, 10s. reward."

(GROCER whistles for ploughman.)

You wait here while I drive on and speak to the ploughman over there.

(GROCER starts to go off stage L.   PIG-WIG wants to move.)

Pigling Bland   Not yet, Pig-wig, he will look back.

(The GROCER looks back.   The two pigs stand stock-still in the road.   The GROCER goes off to speak to ploughman stage L.)

Now, Pig-wig, NOW!

(They turn and run up the road that leads over the hills.   They squeal as they go.   As they come level with the farmhouse, MISS POTTER comes to her gate and speaks to the audience.)

Miss Potter *(smiling)*   Never did any pigs run as these pigs ran!   They raced and squealed and they ran down the hill.   They came to the river, they came to the bridge – they crossed it hand in hand – then over the hills and far away she danced with Pigling Bland!